My Bible AE

GW00870160

Are you ready? It's time to...

Colour

Talk

Ask

Read

Pray

Draw

Play

Look out for Squeak the mouse who appears on every page. See how many Bible verses you can look up. There is a page at the end of the book to record which ones you do.

Written by Catherine Mackenzie - Illustrated by Jane Taylor
Published by Christian Focus Publications
Printed and bound by Bell and Bain, Glasgow

A is for Adam

Adam was the first ever man. Eve was the first ever woman. God made them both. He didn't just make one person, he made two. He realised that Adam would need somebody to be a friend and helper to him. So God made a woman and she was called Eve.

God made the whole world. It was perfect. It was very good. God saw that it was very good. He was pleased. It was a lovely place to live. There was no anger, or pain or sorrow. It was beautiful. Everything was as good as it could be, because God made it. But what happened next? Read on and find out.

You can do it

*   God made you. Thank him for your body.
*   Read Psalm 139:13-16.
*   What colour is your hair?

B is for badness

Badness came into the world. Another name for badness is sin. *God hates sin.* Badness is what some people call sin. Sin is when people disobey God and his commands.

Can you think of some things that people do which are bad? Can you think of some things which you do that are bad? What should you do when you do something bad? You should say sorry to God and ask him to help you to be good next time.

But if God made everything in his world lovely how did Badness come into God's good world? Read on and you will find out.

You can do it

* When you do something bad say sorry to God. Read Acts 17:30.
* Listen to the sounds around you.
* What can you hear?
* What is your favourite sound?

C is for care

When you care for someone you love them. *God loves and cares for you.* God cared for Adam and Eve. God cared for the people he had made. He loved them.

He gave Adam and Eve lots of good things. He gave them beautiful trees with loads of fruit. He gave them birds and animals - big friendly ones and little small bouncy ones. Adam and Eve were not frightened of snakes or lions. The world was a peaceful place. But God gave Adam and Eve one rule. He gave them an instruction to obey. *It is important to obey God.* What was the instruction he gave Adam and Eve? Read on and you will find out.

You can do it

* God made all the animals. Thank God for them.
* Read Genesis 1:20-25.
* What is your favourite animal?

D is for don't

God told Adam and Eve 'Don't eat from that tree'. It is the tree of knowledge of good and evil.'

God warned them, 'You can eat of everything else but don't eat from that tree, or you will die.'

Do you remember if Adam and Eve had other trees that they could eat from? Yes they did! God had given them lots of trees. God had given them lots of lovely fruit and food to eat. *God gave Adam and Eve everything they needed*. So when God told Adam and Eve, 'Don't eat the fruit from that tree,' did they obey this instruction? Read on and find out.

You can do it

*   God tells us to be good to others. Ask God to help you to be good.
*   Read Luke 6:27.
*   What is your favourite food?

E is for Eve

She was the first person to disobey God. The serpent tricked her into eating the fruit. Eve told the serpent, 'God has told us not to touch that fruit or we will die!'. 'You won't die', the serpent lied.

The serpent made Eve think that God hadn't been telling the truth. *God always tells the truth.* Eve looked at the fruit. It looked lovely. She picked a piece and then ate it. Then she told Adam to eat it too. Adam ate the fruit. Everything went wrong. How did Adam and Eve feel now? Read on and find out.

You can do it

* Always tell the truth. It is wrong to lie. Ask God to help you tell the truth.
* Read Exodus 20:16.
* Adam and Eve had lots of fruit to eat. What is your favourite fruit?

F is for friends

When Adam and Eve sinned they were no longer friends with God. Instead of being friends with God, Adam and Eve were now frightened of God. They knew they had done a bad thing. They knew that God hated sin. Instead of being peaceful and happy, they were now frightened, angry and miserable.

Adam and Eve tried to hide from God. But they couldn't do that because *God is everywhere*. They heard him calling for them, so they ran into the garden and hid. But God knew where they were. He found them. What did God do? Read on and find out.

You can do it

* God is everywhere. Thank him for looking after you.
* Read Psalm 139: 7-10.
* Now play hide and seek.
* What is your favourite hiding place?

G is for gave

God gave Adam and Eve clothes to wear. Because they had disobeyed God, they felt ashamed to be without clothes. Adam and Eve felt sad for the first time. God had to give them clothes to cover their bodies.

But God also gave them a punishment. God has to punish sin. Adam and Eve had to leave the special garden that God had made for them. They were not allowed to return. Adam and Eve had to leave it for ever. What would Adam and Eve do now? Read on and you will find out.

You can do it

*   God gave Adam and Eve clothes. Thank God for the clothes that you have.
*   Read Matthew 6:28.
*   What are your favourite clothes? What colours are they?

H is for hard

Adam and Eve had to work very hard. Adam had to dig up lots of weeds, and thorns and thistles. He had to work very hard to get food for them to eat. It was hard and thirsty work. Later Adam and Eve had two little boys. They had to work even harder to feed and clothe their children.

Everything was difficult now. They should not have disobeyed God. They should have listened to him and obeyed him. We should listen and obey God also.

Other horrible things happened too. What were they? Read on and you will find out.

You can do it

*   Thank God for the food you eat.
*   Make a list of the food you ate today.
*   Read Luke 11:3.
*   When you are thirsty what is your favourite drink?

I is for illness

Illness is another horrible thing that came into the world when Adam and Eve disobeyed God. Illness, pain and sadness came into the world because people couldn't obey God.

Adam and Eve sinned first, but all the people that came after them sinned too. All the people before you were born, sinned. And all the people after you, will sin every day of their lives too. The sin just didn't stop. We are all guilty. But God had a rescue plan. He was going to send someone really special to help. Who was that special person? Read on and you will find out.

You can do it

* If you are well say thanks to God.
* If you're ill ask God to help you.
* Read Exodus 15:26.
* Take some toys and make
  - a toy hospital.
* What is your favourite toy?

J is for Jesus

Jesus was God's special person. Jesus was God's rescue plan. When Adam and Eve sinned Jesus hadn't come to earth yet but he was alive in heaven. This is because Jesus is God's son and has never had a beginning. He will never have an end either. He is eternal.

Jesus, God's Son, was God's rescue plan for human beings. When God gave Adam and Eve a punishment he gave them a promise too. God promised to send them a Saviour one day. Who was that Saviour? God's Son was the Saviour... Jesus Christ. Did people stop sinning because they knew God would send them a Saviour? Read on and find out.

You can do it

*   Jesus came to rescue you.
    Thank him for loving you.
*   Read Psalm 91:14.
*   What do you call people who rescue other people from a fire?
*   What do you want to be when you grow up?

K is for kind

People weren't kind. Sin made them nasty. They were hating and fighting and killing. They weren't being kind at all. People were still sinning. But God is kind. He hates sin. God hates it when people fight. He wants people to be kind. You should use your hands to do good things and not nasty things.

Adam and Eve's two sons were called Cain and Abel. Cain was jealous of Abel so he killed him. That was the first murder. It was very, very sad. All the sin in the world is very, very, sad. How does this sin make God feel? Read on and find out.

You can do it

*   Thank God for how kind he is.
*   Read Psalm 86:5.
*   Make a thumb picture. Paint your thumb and press it onto paper. Your thumb is the only thumb in the whole world that looks like this.
*   How loudly can you clap?

L is for love

God is love. Even though people were sinning and being nasty, God still loved the people he had made. He longed for them to be friends with him once more.

But people still sinned. They didn't turn their hearts back to God and love him. People didn't want God in charge even though his ways were best. They preferred to go on hurting and harming other people and themselves. Sin is an awful thing! Isn't it!

Did God decide that he was just going to ignore sin? Of course not! Read on and find out what God did next.

You can do it

*   Thank God that he wants to be your friend.
*   Read Proverbs 18:24.
*   Do you have best friends? Who are they?
*   Write a post-card to your best friend. Tell them that God loves them.

M is for many

God couldn't ignore sin. He hates sin. People kept sinning. Many years later it was still the same. Even after hundreds of years people hadn't changed. People were still wicked and didn't listen to God.

Many people did many bad things. God became so angry with sin that one day he wished he had never thought of making people. He wished he hadn't made people at all. But there was still one man who was different. This man loved God and listened to him. What was this man's name? Turn the page and read the next part of the story. Then you will find out who he is.

You can do it

* Thank God for how fair he is. He is always right.
* Read Deuteronomy 32:4.
* Ask a grown up to cut an apple into pieces. Be fair and share it.
* God made the world. What things do you like to make?

N is for Noah

Noah was the man's name. Noah was a man who listened to God. He wasn't like the other people who ignored God. God told Noah that he was going to destroy the whole earth with a flood, because of the sin of all the people. But Noah and his family and a lot of animals would be saved from the flood.

God told Noah to build a big boat, called an ark, so that he and his family and the animals could be safe from the floods. Everyone inside the ark would survive. Everyone outside the ark would die. Did Noah obey God? Read on and find out.

You can do it

*   God speaks to you in the Bible.
    Thank God for the Bible.
*   Read Psalm 56:4.
*   Ask a grown up to fill a sink with water.
    Take an empty yoghurt pot. Does it float?
    Fill it with pennies? Does it float now?
*   What is your favourite Bible story?

O is for obey

Did Noah obey God? Yes he did. He built an ark. All Noah's family went inside the ark. The animals went inside too. There were lots of them.

When the water covered over all the world, Noah and his family were safe. God kept Noah and his family safe in the ark. When the floods went away Noah and his family and the animals went outside to start again. Noah and his family thanked God for being so good to them.

That was when the rainbow appeared across the sky for the very first time. God made the rainbow as a special sign to human beings that he loved them and would never flood the whole world again.

You can do it

*   We should obey God.
*   Read Deuteronomy 13:4.
*   What colours are in a rainbow?
*   What colours can you see now?
*   What is your favourite colour?

P is for people

People still sinned after the flood. But God knew that they would. That is why he had the best rescue plan ever. Do you remember that God promised Adam and Eve he would send a Saviour? Do you remember who that Saviour was? It was Jesus. Jesus was God's rescue plan. This rescue would be even better than the ark rescue.

People were saved from the flood when they went into the ark. When Jesus came he rescued people too. His rescue was even more amazing because people were saved from hell because of him. What was the special thing that Jesus did? Read on and find out.

You can do it

* You need to be saved from sin. Thank God for sending Jesus to save you.
* Read John 3:16.
* Who rescues sick people when you phone 999?
* What people are in your family? What are their names?

Q is for question

The answer to the question, 'What did Jesus do?' is - Jesus died for our sins. But first of all Jesus came to earth. He was born, he grew up and then he died. But his death was special because when he died it meant that he was taking the punishment that was meant for us.

Perhaps you are asking other questions too? Why was Jesus special? When did he come? What did he do? What was he like? Was he big and strong? Was he rich and powerful? Read on and you will find out the answers to these questions and more.

You can do it

* Thank Jesus for loving you.
* Read Psalm 136:1.
* Find a picture of a baby.
  What do babies do?
  What do parents do for babies?
* Write down the day on which you were born and the year. This is called your birthday.

R is for righteous

Jesus is righteous. Righteous means perfect. Jesus never did anything wrong. Jesus was always right. He never sinned.

Jesus wasn't rich and powerful when he lived on earth. His mum and dad were quite poor. Jesus was born as a tiny baby. He grew taller, he ate food, he slept and did all these things that we do, but he didn't do anything naughty. Jesus was very special. He lived a perfect life and then he died on the cross. Jesus came because he wants to save us from our sins.

What is Jesus special name? Read on and find out.

You can do it

* Thank Jesus that he is perfect and never wrong.
* Read Matthew 5:48.
* How tall are you? If you don't know ask a grown up to help measure you.

S is for Saviour

Saviour was Jesus' special name. It was the special name given to the special person who God sent to the world. Jesus Christ, God's son, was the special Saviour that God sent to earth. Jesus' mother, Mary was told by an angel to give the baby the name Jesus - as he would save people from their sins.

Jesus would save people from their sins when he died on the cross. Jesus died on the cross even though he had done nothing wrong. Jesus died so that one day, the people who believe in him and love him could live in heaven for ever. Do you know what you have to do? Read on and find out.

You can do it

*   Tell Jesus he is special!
*   Read Exodus 15:2.
*   What is your name?
        Who chose your name for you?
        Why did they give you that name?

T is for truth

God always tells the truth. We can trust him. When God speaks to us he uses the Bible. When you speak what do you use? You use your mouth. You should always tell the truth. If you tell lies then that is a sin. It is wrong.

Everything you read about Jesus in the Bible is true. You have to believe that Jesus died for you and that Jesus loves you. Jesus showed love for people all the time. He healed people and taught them about God. He told them that the only way to be friends with God , was to trust in him. Find out what the opposite of trust is by reading the next part of the book.

You can do it

*   God always tells the truth.
  Read Isaiah 45:19.
*   Hide a penny for someone to find.
  Tell the person if they are close or
  far away. Tell them the truth.
*   You speak with your mouth.
  What else does your mouth do?
*   What is your favourite song?

U is for unbelief

Unbelief is the opposite of trust. Some people don't believe in Jesus. It is wrong not to believe in Jesus.

When Jesus spoke to people, some didn't believe what he said. Some people hated him. They wanted to kill him. Jesus' enemies arrested him and accused him of doing things he hadn't done. That was when Jesus was taken away to be killed.

Some of Jesus' best friends left him. One friend, Peter, said that he didn't know Jesus at all. Jesus looked at Peter and knew how nasty he had been. Peter was so sorry he cried. What happened next? Read on and find out.

You can do it

*   Thank God that he tells us about himself.
*   Read Exodus 33:19.
*   White is the opposite of black.
          Can you think of other opposites?
*   When you're sad your eyes cry.
          What else do eyes do?
          What colour are your eyes?

V is for very

It was very sad. Jesus' enemies whipped him, hurt him and they made fun of him. They made Jesus carry a big, heavy cross by himself. He was very tired. Then they took some nails and nailed him to the cross. Jesus felt very sore. It was hot and he was sore and thirsty and tired. It was very painful.

But even when he was feeling very sore - Jesus asked a friend to look after his mother. Jesus even asked his Father, God, to forgive the people who hurt him. Then Jesus died. Some friends buried him in a tomb in a garden. But why did Jesus have to die? Read on and find out.

You can do it

* Jesus died to save us from sin. Say sorry to God for your sins.
* Read 2 Corinthians 5:21.
* Jesus was buried in a garden. What is your favourite flower?
* Jesus prayed for others when he was on the cross. Who do you want to pray for?

W is for world

Jesus came to save the world. When he died it wasn't the end. When Jesus died, it was all part of God's rescue plan.

Jesus' death was God's plan. Sin must be punished. It is so bad, it must be punished by God, with death. But Jesus gave people a second chance. When he died, he died instead of us. If you trust in Jesus and love him, you will go to heaven when you die to be with Jesus for ever. This is because of his great love for you. But was Jesus' death the end of everything? What happened to Jesus after he died? Read on and find out.

You can do it

* Thank God for his perfect plan to save the world and you.
* Read 1 John 2:2.
* What other countries in the world do you know?
* Where do you live? What is your address?

X What is X for?

X doesn't stand for very many words. It looks like a cross though. Jesus died on the cross for you. Don't ever forget that. The letter X is the second letter in some words like eXcellent and eXciting. God is excellent and exciting. But the really excellent part to this story is the story of the resurrection. Did you know that when Jesus died he didn't stay dead forever? When Jesus' friends heard this they were amazed. Peter ran to the garden tomb to see if it was true. And it was. He was very glad. We should be glad too.

Jesus died and rose again, and is now in heaven. He is waiting for someone. Who is he waiting for? Read on and find out

You can do it

*   Draw your hand. On each finger write
    a prayer to God.
*   Read Psalm 6:9.
*   What is your favourite day of the week?
*   Peter ran to the tomb.
    Do you like to run? Can you run fast?
    Jog up and down on the spot.
    See how fast your legs can go.

Y stands for you

Jesus is waiting for you. Jesus is waiting for you to tell him you love him. Jesus is also waiting for that special day when he will come back to earth. That will be the day when sin is destroyed and all those who love Jesus will be in heaven together.

But we don't have to wait for that special day to tell Jesus that we love him. We can tell him now. We can ask God to forgive our sins in Jesus' name - right this very minute.

What is the next letter? Read on and find out.

You can do it

* Heaven is wonderful. Jesus is there.
* Read 1 Peter 3:21-22.
* Ask a grown up to help you make a diary. Write down special days, like birthdays and holidays.
* What do you do on God's day? Is it a special day?
* Draw a sun picture to remind you that God's day is special.

Z is for what?

There are hardly any words beginning with the letter Z either - there are Zoos and Zig Zag and Zap. But there is one thing about the letter Z - It is the very last letter in the alphabet.

So just remember that Jesus should be your first thought when you wake up and your last thought when you go to sleep. Think about how lovely Jesus is. Tell him that you love him. Thank him for his love for you.

You can do it

*   When you wake up and go to sleep you should remember to speak to God.
*   Read Psalm 5:3.
*   When do you wake up and when do you go to sleep?
*   Draw a picture of a clock. Underneath write the word, 'Pray' to remind you to speak to God at anytime.

All about you

What is your name?

Who chose your name for you?

Why did they give you that name?

What day were you born on and in what year?

What colour is your hair?

What colour are your eyes?

Where do you live?

How tall are you?

What is your favourite:

    sound?

    animal?

    food?

    fruit?

    hiding place?

Draw a picture of you

Draw a picture of your favourite animal

What are your favourite clothes? What colours are they?

When you are thirsty what is your favourite drink?

What is your favourite toy?

What is your favourite Bible story?

What is your favourite colour?

What is your favourite song?

What is your favourite flower?

What people are in your family? What are their names?

Do you have some best friends? Who are they?

Who do you want to pray for?

What special days do you like?

What do you do on God's special day?

Is it a special day?

Draw a picture of your favourite Bible Story

What do you want to be when you grow up?

How loudly can you clap your hands?

What things do you like to make?

Do you like running? Can you run fast?

When do you wake up and when do you go to sleep?

Do you pray to God when you wake up in the morning?

Draw a picture of you asleep

Do you pray to God when you go to sleep at night?

What do you want to pray for most of all?

What is your favourite Bible verse?

Draw a picture of the world

All about God

What I have learnt about God in this book

God made the whole world.

God hates sin.

God cares for you and loves you.

It is important to obey God.

Draw a picture of you being good

Draw a picture of the Garden of Eden

God gave Adam and Eve everything they needed.

God always tells the truth.

God is everywhere.

God has to punish sin.

We should listen to and obey God.

God had a rescue plan. He would send someone really special to help. Jesus was God's special person. Jesus was God's rescue plan. God is kind. God is love.

God became so angry with sin that one day he wished he had never thought of making people. God told Noah he would destroy the world with a flood.But God kept Noah and his family safe in the ark.

Draw a picture of Noah and the ark

Draw a picture of a rainbow

God made the rainbow as a special sign to human beings that he loved them and would never flood the whole world again.

Noah's family and the animals were saved from the flood when they went into the ark. When Jesus came he rescued people too. His rescue was even more amazing because people were saved from hell.

Jesus died for our sins. Jesus never did anything wrong. Jesus Christ, God's son, is the special Saviour that God sent to earth. He can be your Saviour too. He is your Lord and your God and you should obey him.

Jesus says, "Let the little children come to me and don't try to stop them! People who are like these little children belong to God's kingdom."
Matthew 19:14.

The different bible verses I have read are:

Psalm 139:13-16 ☐ ☆

Acts 17:30 ☐ ☆

Genesis 1:20-25 ☐ ☆

Luke 6:27 ☐ ☆

Exodus 20:16 ☐ ☆

Psalm 139: 7-10 ☐ ☆

Matthew 6:28 ☐ ☆

Luke 11:3 ☐ ☆

Exodus 15:26 ☐ ☆

Psalm 91:14 ☐ ☆

Psalm 86:5 ☐ ☆

Proverbs 18:24 ☐ ☆

Deuteronomy 32:4 ☐ ☆

Psalm 56:4 ☐ ☆

Deuteronomy 13:4 ☐ ☆

John 3:16 ☐ ☆

Psalm 136:1 ☐ ☆

Matthew 5:48 ☐ ☆

Exodus 15:2. ☐ ☆

Isaiah 45:19 ☐ ☆

Exodus 33:19 ☐ ☆

2 Corinthians 5:21 ☐ ☆

1 John 2:2 ☐ ☆

Psalm 6:9 ☐ ☆

1 Peter 3:21-22 ☐ ☆

Psalm 5:3 ☐ ☆

CHRISTIAN FOCUS

Staying Faithful - Reaching Out!

Christian Focus Publications publishes biblically-accurate books for adults and children. If you are looking for quality Bible teaching for children then we have a wide and excellent range of Bible story books - from board books to teenage fiction, we have it covered. You can also try our new Bible teaching Syllabus for 3-9 year olds and teaching materials for pre-school children.

These children's books are bright, fun and full of biblical truth, an ideal way to help children discover Jesus Christ for themselves. Our aim is to help children find out about God and get them enthusiastic about reading the Bible, now and later in their lives.

www.christianfocus.com

© copyright 2001 Christian Focus Publications Reprinted 2005
ISBN: 1-85792-605-6
Printed and bound by Bell and Bain, Glasgow
Text by Catherine Mackenzie Illustrations by Jane Taylor

Published by Christian Focus Publications, Geanies House, Fearn, Tain, Ross-shire, IV20 1TW, Scotland, UK. All rights reserved. No part of this publication may be reproduced, stored in a retrieval system, or transmitted, in any form or by any means electronic, mechanical, photocopying, recording or otherwise, without prior permission of Christian Focus Publications.

Written for my friends,

Lydia, Esther, Philip, Lois and Jack

with love - Catherine.